63

A VANLIFE GUIDE
TO OUR NATIONAL PARKS

BY BRANDON FORMANACK

Meet the Author

My name is Brandon, and I just made it to all the national parks in the United States! The 63 parks are spread throughout the entire country making this a tough accomplishment. My love of national parks began when I was 13 years old. I went on a family trip to Hawaii in July of 2006. Here I visited my first national park–Hawaii Volcanoes National Park! The Polaroid photo shown below is my first picture taken in a national park while on that trip. In the image there is smoke coming from the lava flowing into the ocean. We did a sunset hike out on the lava field to see the red glow. I was mesmerized at this astonishing phenomenon. That was the moment I started to appreciate national parks.

In high school I was going through my grandparents things that they were getting rid of, and I found a book on the national parks published in 1985. I then learned that my grandma had actually worked in Yellowstone when she was in high school which sparked my interest even more. After graduating college I visited my second national park–Zion! Hiking to Angels Landing (*photographed above*) blew me away with its beauty. This was the moment that set my national park journey in motion. As a Christian, Zion was especially intriguing to me for all the biblical references throughout the park such as the three sandstone peaks named Abraham, Isaac, and Jacob.

Hawaii Volcanoes National Park July 2006

For the next few years I made it a point to visit a few more national parks each year. Then in 2022, I decided to buy a van and convert it into a campervan to use for visiting the parks. It took me a year to fully convert the van while working full time. I then decided to take a year off of work to accomplish my goal of visiting all the national parks. I had saved up money and was making some rental income to support myself for the year. I wanted this experience of getting to hike the parks while I had the physical capabilities of doing everything I wanted to instead of waiting until I retire. Having completed my goal of visiting all 63 parks, I am beyond grateful for the time I was able to spend admiring God's beautiful creation.

About this Book

The National Park System includes 428 different "parks" in the United States. Congress works with the NPS to designate new national parks and determine the status of a park. Of the 428 properties, only 63 are classified as national parks. Examples of other areas include national rivers, monuments, or battlefields.

Any time you see this symbol throughout the book it will signify wildlife seen in the park. This won't include all possible animals that are found in the park—only the animals I personally saw on my visit.

My intention for this book is to inspire others to visit America's beautiful parks. Further, I include helpful information for those traveling in a van since that is what I did. This book goes through the route that I took to visit all 63 of the national parks. Each park is featured throughout the book. For each national park I include photographs and a brief description. If I particularly enjoyed a hike or certain area of a park I make sure to mention that as well. This is by no means a comprehensive guidebook—just a visual story to inspire you to get out and enjoy what our national parks have to offer! Note: all photos were taken from my iPhone.

While visiting national parks I find that the best resource is a free app called "National Park Trail Guide." I love using this app to find out which hikes I want to do. Additionally, this app works with the GPS on your phone to track where you are in the park. This feature is awesome because most of the time there is no cell service in national parks. As long as you don't close the app, the app will show you where you are in the park. While hiking, it will even show you how far you've gone on the trail.

Converting the Van

Bought a 1998 Ford E-150 van that had a wheelchair lift in it..

Stripped out the inside of the van.

Installed insulation and flooring.

Built a bed frame, added solar panels, and installed a sink.

Added siding, a ceiling, storage shelves, and lights.

The finished product!

Vanlife with a Dog

I could not have made it through the journey without my dog, Mako! While traveling with a pet does present some challenges, it was well worth it for me. She was a great companion to have along the journey especially at night since she likes to cuddle. It took her a couple weeks to adjust to living in the van, but she quickly learned to enjoy the new lifestyle. She had a blast exploring all over on hikes and campsites.

One of the biggest concerns I had prior to vanlife was leaving Mako in a hot van while I had to run errands. Knowing this, I painted the roof of my van with a white reflective roof coating to keep the top of the van from absorbing heat. Just like a windshield shade, I custom-made similar shades for all the windows. I also bought a higher grade window tint that blocks out UV rays. Furthermore, I installed an RV fan in the roof of the van. I purchased the most expensive fan, and it was one of the best decisions I made. Thankfully, the van came equipped with three small sliding screen windows. I would open one or two of these windows, and the fan would pull air into the van and out through the top keeping the van cool.

Unfortunately, dogs aren't allowed on a majority of the trails in the National Park System. For the parks that aren't very dog friendly, I would usually plan to go for an early morning or late afternoon hike and park in the shade while she chilled.

As far as dog friendly places go, Roswell, NM was by far the best! Dogs are allowed everywhere–from museums, to cafes, to gift shops. Often in my travels, I would just bring Mako into a store or coffee shop, and no one ever questioned it.

Mako seeing bison for the first time.

Vanlife FAQ

How do you shower?

I got a membership for the year at Planet Fitness. It only cost me $25/month to use any facility in the U.S. or Canada, and they are scattered all over the place. This allows me to use WiFi and the massage chairs too! I also fill up my water bottles at the gym.

What about electricity?

I have solar panels on the roof of the van connected to a separate battery. This allows me to have power in the middle of the wilderness so that I can power things like the lights, refrigerator, fan, water pump, and my phone. I also try to charge things from the cigarette outlet while I'm driving.

How do you cook?

To be honest I don't cook much. I have a fridge so I keep things like fruit, deli meat, hummus, and salads on hand. I do have a single burner gas stove, so I can cook things like hamburgers or eggs & bacon with that. I eat fast food a lot too for the convenience and low expense factor. If I have leftovers or buy a frozen meal, almost every gas station has a microwave to use for reheating food on the road.

Where do you get water?

Underneath my sink I have a 5 gallon container that I would refill at water filter stations outside of grocery stores.

Where do you park for the night?

For me, this is fairly easy. While I do have a lot of stickers on the back of my van, that's the only thing that makes the van look like a camper from the outside. You can barely see the solar panels so most of the time people have no idea I am sleeping in my van, especially since the windows are tinted. Sometimes I find a quiet parking lot, or I park on the street in a nice neighborhood. Ideally I find a spot out in nature with a nice view to enjoy for the night. This is easier to do out west and in Alaska than on the east coast. Most Planet Fitnesses are 24hr, so that is also a great spot. BLM land is a great place for free camping, and I often find these spots using an app called "The Dyrt" or "Campendium."

What's the hardest part of vanlife?

This question stumped me for the longest time because I love living and traveling in a van! Nothing really was hard for me until I had mechanical issues! When the van breaks down—your house breaks down. This happened once in the middle of Yosemite and getting a tow truck took about 7 hours.

My Vanlife Journey

I finished converting the van February of 2023, and then I proceeded to quit my job in March. Since it is still cold in most of the U.S. this time of year, I left my home in Atlanta and headed to Texas. I began with Big Bend National Park since temperatures here would be more mild compared to northern USA. While I also could have gone south to hit the Florida national parks too, I just decided to save those for the end.

I didn't solely visit national parks–I also stopped along the way at some state parks and various roadside attractions along the way. I also took the time to visit friends and family along the way. Not only was it great visiting with loved ones, but it also gave me an opportunity to use their laundry or showers.

I first focused on all the national parks in the region shown on the opposite page. I was especially blown away at the beauty in New Mexico. This is such an underrated state. Not only are there gorgeous landscapes, but the culture in the cities is remarkable. I really enjoyed the architecture in Santa Fe, as well as the campy alien themed town of Roswell. Arizona also has tons of outdoor spots to camp and explore. I stayed in this region for a while as I waited for the warmer weather in the north.

After visiting the Grand Canyon, I began my drive north with Alaska being the goal. I found some amazing spots to explore on the way like the Bonneville Salt Flats outside of Salt Lake City and the 12 Mile hot springs in Nevada. From there I made it to Glacier National Park before crossing into Canada. I will go more in depth about this later, but the drive through the Canadian Rockies was the most scenic drive I've ever experienced.

I arrived in Alaska in early June and stayed for almost five weeks leaving mid July. There were a lot of cold and rainy days in June. If I had done anything different, I would have visited Alaska late summer instead of early summer. However, I was avoiding the heat in the lower 48 during this time which was the goal. Alaska is so vast and full of wilderness to be explored. It was no problem finding spots to park the van for the evening with a view of the mountains. I even took the van to the town of North Pole, AK.

I drove from Alaska to the state of Washington from here and down the west coast. There are so many parks on the way down to San Diego; it truly is incredible how much diverse beauty there is out west. San Diego was where I left my van to fly to Hawaii and American Samoa. Upon the return from Hawaii, I began my journey east hitting the central and northern parks along the way. This was perfect as it allowed me to be in the northeast during fall to see the leaves changing. Of all the places I visited the best leaf peeping I witnessed was in western Pennsylvania.

I made my way south to spend Thanksgiving with family in South Carolina and finished up my national park journey with Florida parks. This was my plan to be in Florida for December to avoid the cold temperatures in the rest of the U.S. at this time. Then on December 8, I made my way to my final national park, Dry Tortugas!

Heading West

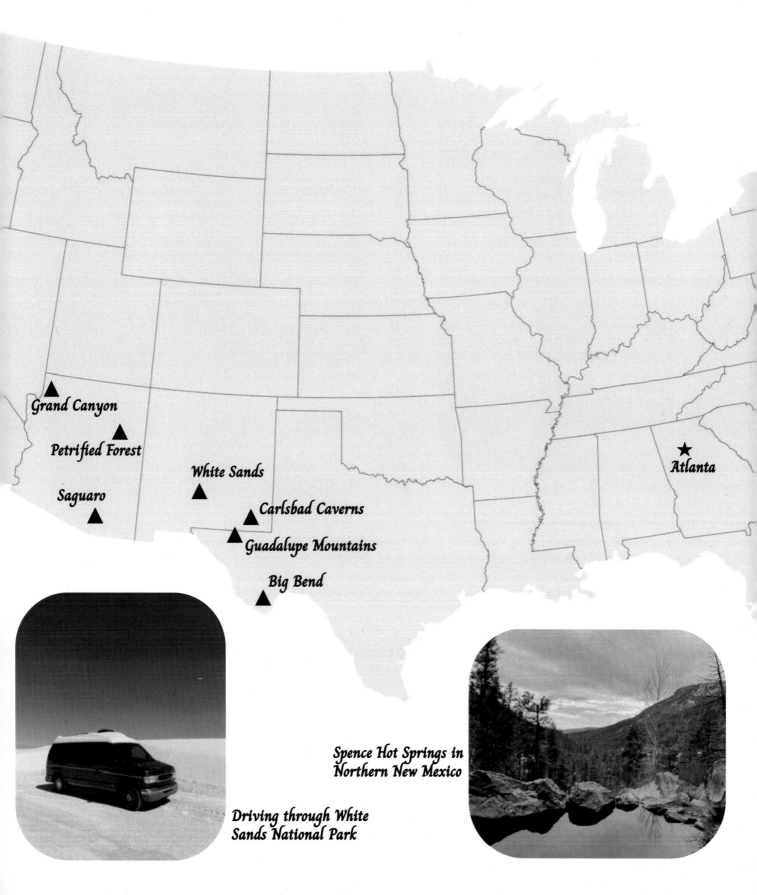

▲ Grand Canyon

▲ Petrified Forest

▲ Saguaro

White Sands ▲

Carlsbad Caverns ▲

▲ Guadalupe Mountains

Big Bend ▲

★ Atlanta

Driving through White
Sands National Park

Spence Hot Springs in
Northern New Mexico

The first park on my vanlife journey! Big Bend is in the middle of nowhere and definitely takes some planning to get here. Located on the Texas / Mexico border, the nearest major city of El Paso is over 4 hours away. The park is located in a desert ecosystem and subject to extreme temperatures. The first day I was at the park it was full sun and close to 100° F, compared to the rain and close to freezing temperatures on the second day. The shape of the Rio Grande river gives the park its name.

My dog, Mako, joined me on this journey through the national parks, and she absolutely loved playing in the Rio Grande river.

 coyote

Boquillas, Mexico

The national park has a U.S. Border entry point that officially goes from the U.S. to this quaint town in Mexico. Don't forget your passport; it is fun to venture over and grab a bite to eat in an authentic Mexican restaurant. You will pay $5 to cross the river via boat & then either walk or ride a donkey into the town!

As I drove up the mountain to this park I was getting nervous as it was snowing, and my van is not 4-wheel drive. Thankfully it was just light snow and getting warmer as the day progressed. The mountain peeks here are very unique compared to the rest of Texas. Compared to Big Bend, this park had significantly fewer visitors which was a welcome solitude. The park has several great day hikes leading to some sweeping views. I spent two days here, and that was a perfect amount of time to explore with Mako.

Highlights:

~ Hike to the Notch via McKittrick Canyon Trail. This is the trail shown on the opposite page.

~ Check out the Gypsum Sand Dunes shown above. Had the dunes all to myself!

Eating lunch in the van with Guadalupe peak towering behind.

GUADALUPE MOUNTAINS
National Park

CARLSBAD CAVERNS
NATIONAL PARK

barbary sheep

As I drove into the park there was an entire herd of sheep in the desert landscape foraging for food. I then proceeded to the visitors center where the cave entrance is located. You need to have a reservation to enter the cave as it fills up. This was by far the coolest cave I've ever been into! What is even better is that you don't have to go with a guide! You enter via the 1.25 mile natural entrance trail which is all downhill. You then can take the flat 1.25 big room loop trail followed by an elevator ride that takes you right back up to the visitor center.

Vanlife Tip

In between Guadalupe Mountains and Carlsbad Caverns there are several free camping areas on BLM land. I boon-docked at a campsite that was called Sunshine Reef. I absolutely recommend it.

White Sands National Park is such a unique and stunning landscape. I definitely enjoyed taking Mako out into the sand dunes to run around. This park is dog friendly which was perfect for us. There are several trails in the dunes which have these markers guiding the way. I decided to head over to the Alkali Flat Trail which is a 5 mile loop trail, which I chose because it was less crowded. I only hiked part of the trail before wandering off to find some solitude in the  dunes for us. Getting lost is very easy to do as the dunes are hard to walk in, and it's uncommon to see people go off trail. To avoid intense heat and strong winds I suggest going early morning when the park opens. For those in a van, the Walmart parking lot nearby was a good place to park for the night.

White Sands
National Park

National Park Service | U.S. Department of the Interior

PETRIFIED FOREST
NATIONAL PARK

UNITED STATES DEPARTMENT OF THE INTERIOR
NATIONAL PARK SERVICE

This national park is very underrated! While the park is known for its large deposits of petrified wood, there is so much more to the park than that. The sheer volume of how much petrified wood that is scattered throughout the landscape is breathtaking. There are tons of unique geological features making it an amazing place to hike or simply drive through. Many of the best sites are easily accessed from the main road. I especially like that this park is so dog friendly.

Highlights:

~ Blue Mesa Trail
~ Crystal Forest
~ Agate Bridge
~ Jasper Forest Overlook

Petrified Forest National Park is one of the few national parks where you can find petroglyphs in the rock face. The image you see here is called Newspaper Rock.

Saguaro National Park is conveniently located in Tuscon, Arizona. The park is divided into two sections on both the east and west sides of Tuscon. For me, a day spent at the park was the perfect amount of time. There are some easy hikes that will take you through the towering saguaro cacti forests.

I highly recommend avoiding the park in the summer as the desert atmosphere can be extremely hot and dry. Going in the spring or fall is the perfect time of year to visit.

Dogs are only permitted on the paved areas of the park.

I recommend exploring the Western Tucson district in the morning before heading into Tuscon for a late lunch. Afterwards, head into the East Rincon mountain district for a late afternoon/evening hike and enjoy sunset from here (*shown above*). Even if you don't hike, the Cactus Forest Loop scenic drive is especially striking at sunset.

rattlesnake

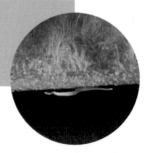

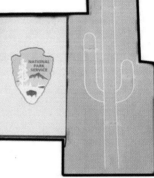

Saguaro
National
Park

Did you know the grand canyon is one of the seven natural wonders of the world? The canyon expands 227 miles carved out by the Colorado River at the base.

ELK

The grand canyon is truly a wondrous creation. Whether you stand on the edge of the cliff and peer down the canyon walls, or raft down the Colorado River and look up at the towering rock faces, it truly is breathtaking. You can access the national park at both the north and south canyon rims.

GRAND CANYON NATIONAL PARK

HAVASUPAI FALLS

Located within the grand canyon lies a desert oasis. A series of crystal clear waterfalls emerge from springs flowing out of the ground. I was sure that the images on social media were too good to be true, but after seeing the blue water in person, I realized that it is even better than the photos! The blue just pops against the sand and stone surroundings.

After seeing two main waterfalls while hiking I arrived at Beaver Falls (*shown on the bottom right*). Beaver Falls is a great place to relax and enjoy a natural water park. This oasis is in the grand canyon, however it is on the Havasupai reservation. To experience this haven you must obtain a permit good for 3 nights camping, and it will cost you about $450. Getting here requires a 10 mile journey into the canyon and back up again on the way out. If backpacking seems too difficult, you can either hire a donkey to carry your bag or helicopter down to the village.

Horseshoe Bend

Nearby Excursions

Two picture perfect sites to see near Grand Canyon National park are Horseshoe Bend (*opposite page*) and Lake Powell (*shown here*).

Lake Powell is a perfect spot to boat or kayak.

Horseshoe Bend offers an unparalleled grand vista of the Colorado River.

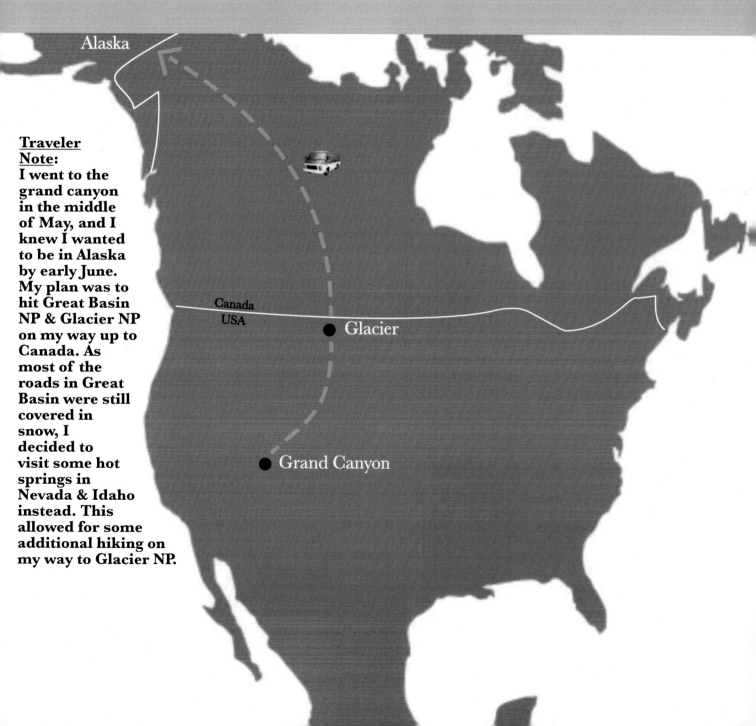

Alaska

Traveler Note:
I went to the grand canyon in the middle of May, and I knew I wanted to be in Alaska by early June. My plan was to hit Great Basin NP & Glacier NP on my way up to Canada. As most of the roads in Great Basin were still covered in snow, I decided to visit some hot springs in Nevada & Idaho instead. This allowed for some additional hiking on my way to Glacier NP.

Canada
USA

Glacier

Grand Canyon

moose, fox, mountain goat

One of my favorite spots in the entire park was called *Goat Lick Overlook*. Here you can see dozens of goats scurrying on the rock face consuming mineral deposits from the soil. Not only are goats common in the park, but there is also a high likelihood of spotting bears. I've talked to a lot of friends who have seen grizzlies here, but sadly I didn't see any at the park.

GLACIER NATIONAL PARK

If you are looking for a great place to camp for the night, I found this awesome spot right on Bear Creek. It is located off Highway 2 shortly after you pass Goat Lick Overlook. It isn't designated as a campsite, but it is in Flathead National Forest and is a river access point. I loved waking up and having my coffee with this view in the morning.

Vanlife Tip

Glacier is a beautiful park and with it comes the crowds. I have heard numerous people say that this is their favorite park. I am not particularly fond of crowds, so I decided to come in late May before the summer masses. It definitely wasn't crowded, but the weather wasn't great. It was sunny the first evening but rained the rest of the time. The scenic Going-to-the-Sun road was still closed because of snow as were the trails I really wanted to hike. I want to come back in September next time. Keep in mind that during summer the park operates on a reservation system for entry, so make sure and plan ahead!

Banff National Park

While this national park is in Canada, I just had to include it in this book. Banff National Park is gigantic and full of spectacular lakes and mountains. A lot of the lakes in the park have a deep blueish gray color as a result of glacial runoff. It is an absolute must see if you have the opportunity. About an hour drive from Calgary is the town of Banff complete with shops, restaurants, and lodging. I have also been to Banff in the winter, and it is the best place I have ever snowboarded!

Alcan Highway

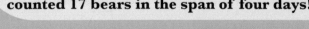

One of the most asked questions I get is what was my favorite spot along my journey. While that is a tough question to answer, it might just be my week long drive along the Alaskan-Canadian Highway! I was honestly dreading it as my GPS told me it would take about 46 hours to get from Calgary to Anchorage, but boy was I mistaken. It turned out to be absolutely gorgeous and teeming with wildlife. It was mountain after lake after mountain after lake for the entire journey with so many beautiful places to camp in solitude! Mako loved exploring the vast wilderness of the Canadian rockies with me. I was worried about gas and food, but there were plenty of options along the way. As for the wildlife, I counted 17 bears in the span of four days!

Katmai Brown Bear

Getting There

Fairbanks

Anchorage

Juneau

From Fairbanks

- 90 min flight to Gates of the Arctic NP
- 3 hour drive to Denali
- 3 hour drive to Wrangell-St. Elias Visitors Center

From Anchorage

- 2 hour drive to Kenai Fjords NP
- 1 hour flight to Lake Clark NP
- 1 hour flight to King Salmon to access Katmai NP
- 2 hour flight to Kotzebue: gateway to Kobuk Valley NP
- 4 hour drive to Denali NP
- 3 hour drive to Wrangell-St. Elias Visitors Center

From Juneau

- 30 min flight, or 3 hour ferry to Glacier Bay NP

Kenai Fjords was my first Alaskan park, and it did not disappoint! This park has the best of both worlds–land & sea. Exit Glacier is the only official trail that you can hike, and you can easily drive there. The hike all the way to the top of the icefield is worth the effort; just beware of avalanche warnings. There are shorter hikes to see the glacier up close at the base.

In order to see a larger portion of the park, you will need to access it by boat. There are multiple companies offering tours of the tidewater glaciers and coastal marine life. I chose to go with *Kenai Fjords Tours* for the price point, and I was very pleased with their service. We had a rough day at sea so be prepared for seasickness. The amount of marine wildlife we saw was stellar! The highlight was seeing a pod of orcas swim by.

 black bear, marmot, bald eagle, puffin, orca, humpback whale, stellar sea lion, sea otter, dalls porpoise, harbor seal

Best Hike:
Harding Icefield Trail (8.2 mi)

Kenai Fjords
National Park

National Park Service
U.S. Department of the Interior

America's largest national park! This was my favorite park in Alaska. For me, the highlight was hiking on a glacier for the first time! I had picked up some crampons from the thrift store, & they worked perfectly for trekking on Root Glacier. I had heard about blue pools, but it was so amazing to see one in person that I had to take a polar plunge in the crystal clear blue water!

You can drive to this national park via two dirt roads. McCarthy road meanders for just over 60 miles to the quaint town of McCarthy which offers lodging & restaurants. From here you can access the abandoned copper mines of Kennecott and the Root Glacier. The other road, Nabesna, runs for just over 40 miles. I took my van all the way down to McCarthy without difficulty. I only drove on Nabesna Road about halfway but never ran into rough terrain. Even though it's longer and further out of the way, I suggest the McCarthy road if you only have time for one. The park was extremely dog friendly which I loved!

moose

Blue Pool on Root Glacier

Lake Clark
National Park and Preserve

Lake Clark National Park is an expansive wilderness. Here the bears thrive off the salmon and vegetation in the park. Many different animals call this park home including a unique species of seals that live in the fresh waters here.

Flying into the park gives a great overview of the vastness of this park. After stopping at the visitor center for advice, my buddy and I began our backpacking journey through the wilderness until we reached the backcountry camping area 3 miles away. As we were the only ones camping out there we experienced a real sense of solitude. Near the camping area there were some kayaks that appeared to be left by the park service for anyone to use. It was very peaceful taking the kayak out on the glassy lake.

The next day we stopped by Tanalian Falls and attempted to hike to the top of Tanalian Mountain. We could see that the dense clouds at the top would prevent any views, so we elected to turn around.

At most parks in Alaska, I carried my bear spray with me for any hiking or camping just in case. Thankfully I never had to use it!

 bald eagle, moose

The only way into Lake Clark National Park is by plane or boat. Lake & Pen Air provides daily flights between Anchorage and the Port Alsworth visitors center for $480 roundtrip.

Sunrise over Kontrashibuna Lake

Getting to Kobuk Valley

Fly from Anchorage to Kotzebue

Step foot in the Arctic Ocean in Kotzebue

Fly from Kotzebue to Ambler

Raft from Ambler to Kiana

Kobuk Valley National Park

This was by far the most difficult park to get to. It required a lot of planning & flexibility. In my opinion, the cheapest & best way to experience the park is to raft from Ambler to Kiana. We rafted along the river for 3 nights and 4 days by camping on sand bars at the edge of the river. I was nervous, but it turned out to be an amazing experience. Two gorgeous mountain ranges surround the valley. Apart from the river, the other draw in the valley is the sand dunes. We flew over the sand dunes on the way to Ambler & honestly were not impressed. So when conditions weren't great for hiking to the dunes, we opted to forgo the dunes and keep rafting.

Grizzly Bear Track

 arctic wolf, moose

As dark as it gets. This photo shows the summer night sky up in the arctic circle. Be prepared for 24 hours of daylight.

 grizzly bear, arctic squirrel, caribou, Dall sheep

Go check out the sled dog kennels & learn more about how they use huskies in the winter to travel through the park.

The park has one main road that is 92 miles one way. As a visitor you can only drive to mile marker 15. To see the rest of the park, you will need to purchase a ticket to take one of the park buses. The tour buses are more expensive and give a more in depth commentary of the park. This is great if you don't plan to hike. For those wanting to hike, the cheaper option is the bus that allows you to hop on and off at your leisure and hike wherever you want. The bus driver still provides park information during the ride.

DENALI
NATIONAL PARK AND PRESERVE

   Mount Denali, formerly Mt. McKinley, stands high in the sky as the tallest mountain in North America. Most visitors to the park never see the mountain as it is above the clouds. I was in Alaska for 5 weeks and I never got a glimpse of it's snowcapped summit. The park is huge and there is no shortage of mountain peaks otherwise.

   While there are some trails in the park, I suggest grabbing a can of bear spray, don some pants, put on your sturdy hiking books, and set off to find your own trail with your daypack. There is so much wilderness in the park begging to be explored. While the visitors center is congested, solitude is not far away.

National Park Service
U.S. Department of the Interior

Brooks Camp

Katmai National Park
and Preserve

Beware! You're in bear country! Come to this park in July, and it's not if, but when, you will see your first bear. Every summer the bears congregate along the Brooks River as the Sockeye salmon migrate up the river to spawn. With millions of salmon running up the river, there is no shortage of food for the bears. Seeing a bear catch a salmon in the river was wild!

Hike: *Dumpling Mountain Trail* **for a great view of of the park**

Getting to this park is not cheap, but it is worth every penny! The only way into the park is by air. From Anchorage, you can arrange a day trip and have a direct flight into the park, but a more affordable option is to take an Alaskan Airline flight from Anchorage to King Salmon. From there you can then either take the ferry or a float plane into Brooks Camp. An advantage of the float plane is that it provides a great view of the park from above. After arrival to Brooks Camp you can either reserve a stay in a campground (surrounded with an electric bear fence) or a room at the lodge. Two days is a great amount of time to explore this park.

brown bear, salmon, bald eagle

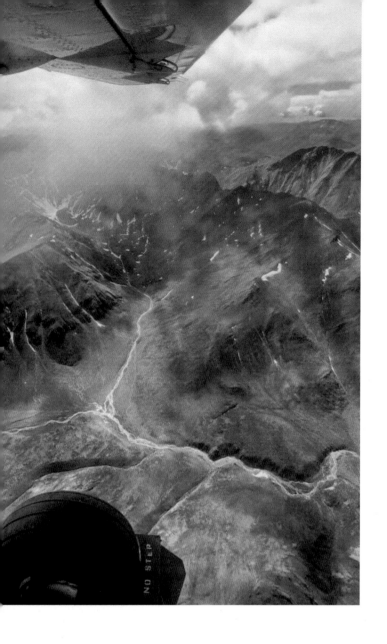

GATES OF THE ARCTIC
NATIONAL PARK AND PRESERVE

Known as the gateway into the arctic, this park is truly rugged. From the moment you step foot into the park, you can get a sense of how wild this park can be. I was greeted by a native who informed me that a week prior a backpacker had been mauled by a grizzly. Thankfully, we had our bear spray & a mobile electric fence to put around the tent while we slept.

There are no trails in the park, and the hiking is not easy. In the summer, this arctic tundra landscape becomes wet and boggy, making forward progression very slow.

You can drive the Dalton Highway, park, and cross both a river and mountain range to hike into the park. After seeing this from the plane I'm glad we didn't choose this route. We opted for roundtrip flights into Anaktuvuk Pass with Wright Air. Charter flights allowing you to go elsewhere in the park are available but will cost considerably more.

According to the park website, 97% of the park visitors never step foot in the park. Most tourists visit the park on a cruise ship, and that is my recommendation. I wanted to really experience the park, so I drove the van to Haines, Alaska. Then, took the car ferry to Gustavus via Juneau. This allowed me to spend 2 nights in the park in the van and keep Mako with me. Besides a cruise ship or a private vessel, there is one operator that offers an all day boat tour of the bay. We only made it about 30 minutes from the dock before the boat engine broke down. In a park with over 1,000 glaciers—I saw none. On top of that, the hiking was pretty subpar compared to the rest of Alaska. Two weeks later, my mom took a cruise, and the ship got right up near the Glacier. Having made the trek to the park on foot, I can't say it's worth the hassle of getting there that way—just book the cruise…it'll be cheaper and nicer.

Glacier Bay National Park actively works on preserving the heritage of the native tribes that have inhabited the area for hundreds of years. Totem poles here represent the Tlingit tribe.

Bald eagle

Humpback whale

Stellar sea lion

Puffin

Glacier view from a cruise ship

Redwoods National Park

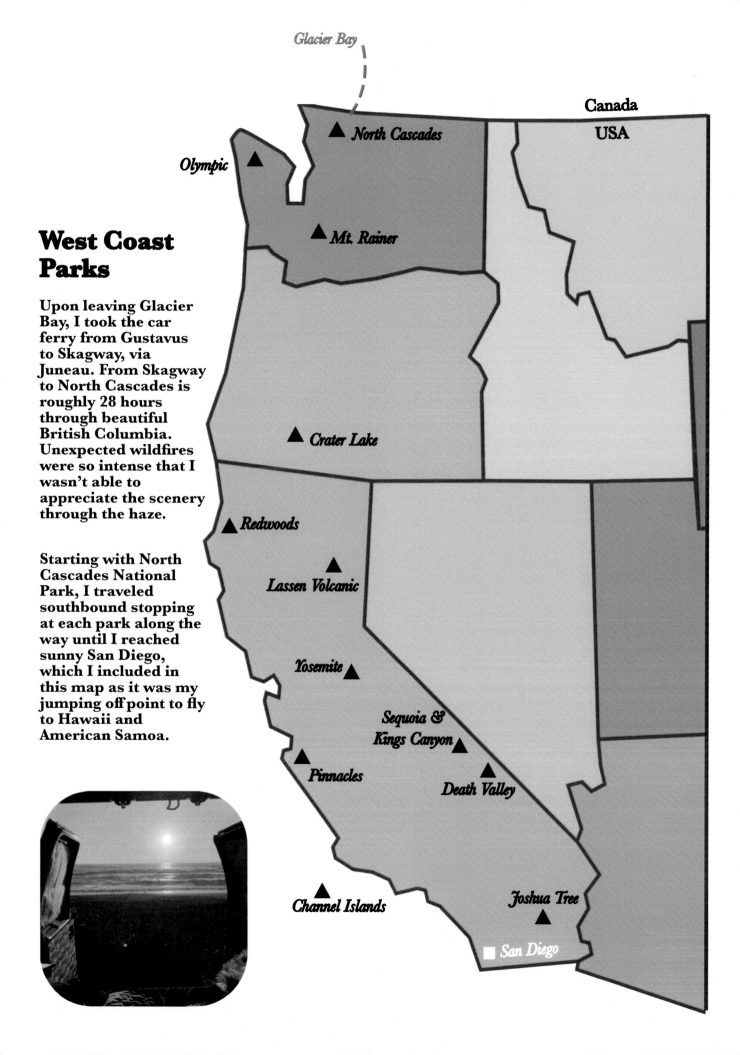

Glacier Bay

North Cascades

Olympic

Canada

USA

West Coast Parks

Mt. Rainer

Upon leaving Glacier Bay, I took the car ferry from Gustavus to Skagway, via Juneau. From Skagway to North Cascades is roughly 28 hours through beautiful British Columbia. Unexpected wildfires were so intense that I wasn't able to appreciate the scenery through the haze.

Crater Lake

Starting with North Cascades National Park, I traveled southbound stopping at each park along the way until I reached sunny San Diego, which I included in this map as it was my jumping off point to fly to Hawaii and American Samoa.

Redwoods

Lassen Volcanic

Yosemite

Sequoia & Kings Canyon

Pinnacles

Death Valley

Channel Islands

Joshua Tree

San Diego

North Cascades
National Park

After visiting all 63 national parks in the U.S., this was my favorite one. It was just stunning everywhere I went, but without the crowds. I honestly didn't know much about the park before going, so when I got here I was blown away with the jagged mountain peaks, glaciers, and blue lakes.

Best Hike:

Cascade Pass to Sahale Arm

The hike is 11.2 miles roundtrip to the glacier. Below is one of the stunning views you will get on this hike! If you want to hike on the glacier then be sure to bring crampons. It was a hot summer day when I went, so I took a side trip down to Doubtful Lake to hop in which was magical!

 mountain goat

Welcome
ʔənʔá čʼə́yəxʷ
Olympic
National Park

Olympic National Park has a wide range of habitats from lakes, to mountains, to ocean, to rainforest. My first stop was the Hurricane Ridge visitors center to experience the mountainous region of the park. Following this, I descended to the beautiful Lake Crescent (photographed above) for a polar plunge in the crystal clear waters. There are several great waterfall hikes in the area that I enjoyed hiking to as well. I then made my way to hike in the Ho Rainforest area before watching a beautiful sunset on the park's coastal region.

 elk, orca whale

UNITED STATES
DEPARTMENT OF INTERIOR
MOUNT RAINIER
NATIONAL PARK

Enjoying a great view of Mt. Rainier from Bench Lake

If you've ever been to Seattle you know how impressive Mount Rainier looks from a distance! When you are in the park, you can see the glaciers up close and marvel at how impressive they are. There are so many great hikes at this park, but here are my two favorites:

Bench & Snow Lake Trail (2.3 mi)

This trail offers gorgeous views of Mt. Ranier with its reflection off Bench Lake.

Grove of the Patriarchs (.9 mi)

After crossing the suspension bridge, you will encounter trees which are over 1,000 years old.

Crater Lake National Park

Sunset view from the van

View from a plane

Cliff diving into the deepest lake in the USA

No matter where you go along the rim of the crater, you will have an amazing view of the water. The park is located at a higher elevation, and access to the park is limited in the winter.

I arrived to the park late afternoon on my first day, and it was wonderful as most of the visitors were leaving! The next day, I saw how crowded the park can get.

My favorite activity was jumping into the bone chilling water of Crater Lake.

Best Hike: Cleetwood Cove Trail
This is the only trail that leads down to the lake (2.2 miles).

Toketee Falls

Van Life Tip

Nearby Crater Lake is Umpqua Hot Springs. It was great to soak in the natural waters after hiking. This was also the perfect parking lot to camp for the night!

Redwoods
National Park

BIG TREE	FEET	METERS
HEIGHT	286	87.2
DIAMETER	23.7	7.2
CIRCUMFERENCE	74.5	22.7
ESTIMATED AGE	1500 YEARS	

 Banana Slug, Elk

These brightly colored insects play a critical role in the ecosystem of the area. The slugs feed on debris and help decomposition take place. This in turn provides the essential nutrients needed by the trees.

Not only is there a forest full of the world's tallest trees, but the park also offers beautiful coastline.

My dog Mako loved running up & down the sandy beach.

It was amazing walking along trails with the world's tallest trees towering all around me. The national park works with state parks to create one giant park here. I highly recommend driving on the scenic Howland Hill Road in Jedediah Smith State Park. While on this drive, stop to hike **Stout Memorial Grove** or **Mill Creek Trail** for stunning trails surrounded by redwoods.

I was fascinated by this tree that the national park turned into a tunnel along **Tall Trees Grove** trail (4.5 miles roundtrip). A free permit is required to hike it which I highly recommend.

Plan for a full day at this park. If time allows, I would spend two days to be able to see everything. Coming from Sacramento, I entered at the Southwest entrance station. In this area of the park you will see volcanic activity from boiling mud pots to steam vents. If you want to climb to the summit of **Lassen Peak**, go early before it gets too hot. This hike is 5 miles roundtrip and offers spectacular views. At the end of the scenic highway is Manzanita Lake where you can get a great view of Lassen Peak. My favorite hike was in the Butte Lake area of the park; the **Cinder Cone** trail is the most unique hike I did in all of the national parks. It might look like that trail up is easy, but with every step you take forward, the cinder rocks pull you backwards. It's a must do for any hiking enthusiast!

View of the volcanic crater from the top

Whether you see Yosemite from the valley or on top of the mountain, it is simply breathtaking. This photograph featured below is one of my favorite spots in Yosemite: Glacier Point. From here you will get an amazing view of the entire park. I really wanted to hike half dome, however spots are limited, and you must apply for a permit via the lottery system in the spring. Unfortunately I did not secure a spot. However there are plenty of other amazing hikes in the park. If you go in the summer expect major crowds. Unless you arrive early in the morning, you can expect wait times of up to 3 hours just to enter the park. You will then struggle to find a parking spot depending on where you plan to go within the park.

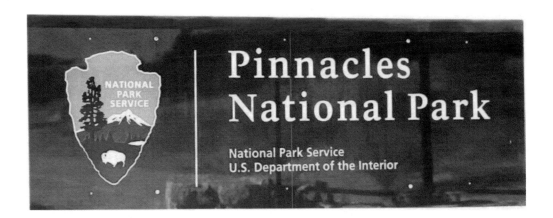

 California condor

A species once on the verge of extinction now thrives at Pinnacles National Park. The California condor is the largest bird in America. If you go in the morning, you will have a better chance of seeing these majestic avians soaring around the higher elevation areas of the park.

Pinnacles makes for a great day trip from San Francisco. I recommend hiking early as the heat is unbearable in the afternoon. There are so many trail segments that connect making it easy to customize your hike. I chose the 5.1 mile **High Peaks** loop that begins at the Bear Gulch Picnic Area. I also loved taking the side trail through **Bear Gulch Cave**. This allows you to venture through the underground passageways. Make sure to bring a headlamp as it gets dark inside!

King's Canyon is home to the 3rd largest tree (by volume) in the world–the **General Grant** tree. You won't want to miss walking through a hollowed out Sequoia tree that fell years ago along the short path leading to the Gen. Grant tree. Due to a landslide, I wasn't able to access most of the park since highway 180 was closed for the entirety of 2023. For me, the park was a little underwhelming since I only got to see a small portion. Other than the trail to see the Gen. Grant tree, none of the other hikes I did were notable.

SEQUOIA NATIONAL PARK

Congress Trail

Congress Trail winds 1.9 miles through some of the largest trees in the entire world. Two famous clusters of sequoia trees stand together forming what is known as the **House** and the **Senate**. In this loop stands the **President**, **Chief Sequoyah**, and the **McKinley** trees. This was one of my favorite trails in the park. A short walk away from the Congress Trail stands the world's largest tree, **General Sherman**. Estimated at over 2,200 years old, this tree is 275 feet tall. While this park contains the largest trees in the world, there are significantly older sequoia trees growing in other parts of the world. Although the trees here are younger, the habitat is more conducive to quicker growth.

Sequoia National Park

Even though the park is known for its collection of giant sequoias, there are plenty of other scenic spots. **Moro Rock** has an amazing 360° view—the perfect reward after ascending 400 stairs to reach the top. Nearby you can actually drive through the sequoia tree tunnel! The van was unfortunately too tall, but it was neat to watch other cars drive through. My favorite hike in the park is the **Lakes Trail**. You will hike to four beautiful alpine lakes. Plan for a full day as the hike is 12.4 miles roundtrip. Don't let the distance deter you as the views along the hike are absolutely amazing. For those looking for a van spot for the night, I parked at the trailhead for the Lakes Trail, and no one disturbed me even in peak season. This was convenient for an early start for my hike before it got too hot.

Pear Lake

What a truly awe-inspiring place! This remains one of my favorite parks for the diversity of the landscape. Avoid traveling here in the summer! Death Valley is the hottest place in the world! On top of that the picturesque **Badwater Basin** is the lowest point in the USA at 282 feet below sea level. Furthermore, its the driest place in the country. I definitely enjoyed the tent camping here. Be prepared for cold and windy conditions overnight.

This national park is huge and contains so many unique landscapes to hike on! From the salt flats to the mountains to the **Mesquite Flats Sand Dunes**. I thoroughly enjoyed hiking on the sand dunes in the park with the mountains all around me. Featured above is what's called the **Artist's Palette**.

This might be my favorite spot to hike in the park. The erosion here leaves colorful pastel mounds of sediment that is beautiful to view when the sun is shining off the soil.

DEATH VALLEY

NATIONAL PARK

Channel Islands National Park

limuw – Santa Cruz Island

National Park Service
U.S. Department of the Interior

Before going to this park, I had low expectations, but I found the ferry ride over and the island hiking to be great! There are 8 channel islands off the coast of Los Angeles, and the national park spans across 5 of them. Accessible by boat or plane, they offer amazing hiking, SCUBA diving, camping, and much more. I saw so much wildlife especially on the ferry to the park. I only stepped foot on the island of Santa Cruz and hiked all the way from **Scorpion Anchorage** to **Yellowbanks Vista**.

humpback whale, fin
whale, common
dolphin, sea lion,
pelican, fox

This park is such a gem in Southern California. For those who want to escape city life for the weekend and camp in the wilderness, it's the perfect spot. While you can see Joshua trees all throughout the region, I really enjoyed the sites this park has to offer. There are some distinctly shaped rocks like **Heart Rock** or **Skull Rock**. Pictured to the right is the scenic **Cholla Cactus Garden**. This is a great trail to get some close up views of the cacti with the mountains in the background. If you like bouldering or rock scrambling, then this is the perfect park for you. There are plenty of spots to climb around the big rock formations throughout the park.

Camp at Jumbo Rocks!

Most national park campgrounds are nice just for the convenience of being in the park. While I usually never paid to camp in a national park, I highly recommend this campground and certain sites to be specific. You'll likely need a reservation to camp here, so I would suggest sites 67, 80, 81, 90, or 119.

Coming here as a teenager and seeing the bright red lava flow into the ocean was so neat; I will never forget it so coming back to this park as an adult and not seeing any lava was definitely less thrilling. It was fascinating to see how the landscape had changed over the years from the volcano. There is always the chance to see lava at the park, so it's just a matter of timing! Good luck!

Whether you are lucky enough to see lava or not, you can still see volcanic activity from the steam vents coming out of the ground. There are several hikes that will take you past some of these vents. Furthermore, taking the path through the lava tube is not to be missed! Definitely drive the **Chain of Craters Road** down to view the **Holei Sea Arch**. On the way down, I enjoyed hiking on the half mile **Devastation Trail**.

Thurston Lava Tube (1.5 mi loop)

HALEAKALĀ
NATIONAL PARK

Sliding Sands Trail

This trail begin at the summit right next to the visitors center. I immediately started the hike after sunrise to avoid the intense heat that is drawn in by the dark colored lava rock. This trail goes for miles, so go as far as you want and then head back. The other option is to leave one car at the bottom and then do a one-way hike down through the crater. This was my favorite trail!

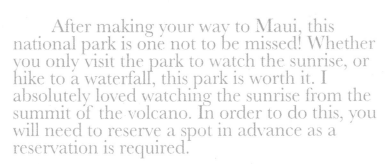

After making your way to Maui, this national park is one not to be missed! Whether you only visit the park to watch the sunrise, or hike to a waterfall, this park is worth it. I absolutely loved watching the sunrise from the summit of the volcano. In order to do this, you will need to reserve a spot in advance as a reservation is required.

In order to see the waterfalls and coastal area of the park, you will need to drive all the way around the volcano to the other side. This part of the park is called the Kipahulu area. Here you can explore along the coast or hike the 3.7 mile **Pipiwai Trail** to see the impressive **Waimoku Falls**.

National Park of American Samoa

Paka Fa'asao o Amerika Samoa

National Park Service
U.S. Department of the Interior

While it's one of the least visited national parks, American Samoa is certainly worthy of being a national park. I spent two days hiking in the park and only saw one other hiker the entire time. Located in the South Pacific, this park takes a long time to get to and requires a lot of planning. The American Samoan islands really aren't set up for tourism, so you will have to be flexible with your travel plans. This also means you will most likely have the beaches all to yourself.

The park is divided up among three islands, however getting to more than just Tutuila will mean that you will have to plan for more than a week spent in the Samoan Islands as travel between islands is very limited. Hiking through the rainforest you will see lots of fruit bats flying in the sky. Expect both sun and rain in the same afternoon and warm temperatures all year round. My favorite spot on the entire island is the **Lower Sauma Ridge Trail** as seen in the photograph to the left. This 1 mile trail leads to the best view on the island.

 fruit bat

Capitol Reef National Park

Heading East

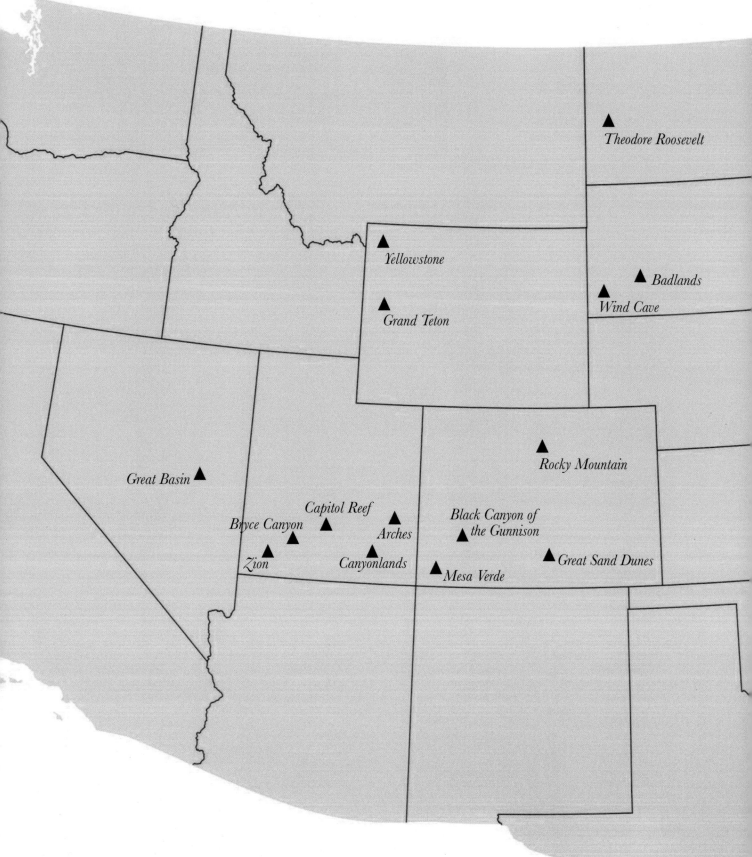

Located in a remote part of Nevada, this park wasn't very crowded during my visit. I enjoyed the **Wheeler Peak Scenic Drive** on the way to hike towards **Rock Glacier**. This roundtrip hike is 4.2 miles long starting on the **Bristlecone Grove Trail** followed by **Glacier Trail**. You will get a great view of Wheeler Peak & Rock Glacier as photographed below. On the return, take the side spur hike to see the crystal clear **Teresa Lake**. Also in the park is **Lehman Caves**; however, I was unable to secure a reservation for the tour.

tarantula

Zion will always be one of my favorite national parks. The feeling I get when I am standing in the canyon is incredible. There are so many amazing spots at this park. The premier hike, **Angels Landing**, is not for the faint of heart. You will use the chains provided to climb your way up the long narrow strip of rock to make it to the top. Because of its popularity, a permit is required to hike all the way to the top. Photographed to the left is the astonishing view you will have once you reach the summit.

For those who love a sense of adventure, considering hiking **The Narrows**. This hike takes place in the river. You will be wading anywhere from ankle deep to chest deep depending on how much rain has occurred recently. Either start at the bottom and hike as far up the river as you want and head back, or get a camping permit and arrange to be dropped off at the top and do a one way hike down the Virgin River. This option will require 16 miles down the river, with a camping spot at the halfway mark.

I love coming to Zion in the fall. It's the best time of year for hiking and you will also experience less crowds.

Zion in Winter

While hiking in the cold isn't always fun, I absolutely loved visiting Zion in the snow! The white blanket of snow is striking against the red canyon walls. Zion can be very congested in peak season, so coming in the winter will offer some solitude in the park. If you decide to hike Angels Landing in the snow, be sure to bring crampons for your boots. If winter doesn't seem appealing to you, then consider exploring the **Kolob Canyon** region of the park for less crowds in peak season. I always enjoy exploring this section of the park as well.

Bryce Canyon
National Park

This park is great for those who just want to drive and hop out for an easy view. On the other hand, hiking down into the canyon offers the chance to explore between all the hoodoos. For a less busy trail, my favorite is the **Peek-A-Boo Loop Trail**. It will take you down into the canyon through an arch.

Both times that I've been to Bryce Canyon, I have been amazed by its beauty. The first time I got a campsite and set up a tent. I had never seen stars as clearly as I did that night. Seeing the entire milky way and shooting stars was amazing. Waking up the next morning to a double rainbow across the canyon was spectacular.

There are so many great hikes in the park. Known for its iconic rock formations that resemble our nation's capitol building, the park has lots of unique landscapes. The photo to the right looked like the jaws of a dinosaur to me. **Cassidy Arch** trail offers some amazing vistas if you are looking for one hike.

This park is way out in the middle of nowhere. I suggest a full day to really enjoy some of the great hiking here. Definitely drive on the 8 mile scenic drive, then continue to **Capitol Gorge**.

Driving through Capitol Gorge

Arches National Park has over 2,000 natural arches within the park borders. While there are so many beautiful spots in the park, a must do is the 3 mile **Delicate Arch** hike photographed on the opposite page. To see a lot all at one place, check out **The Windows** section of the park. This park requires reservations for admission–so plan ahead!

Arches
National Park

Est. 1971

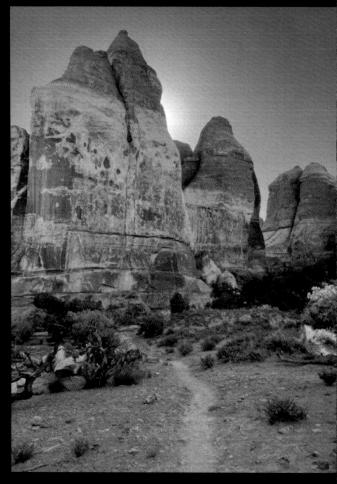

Canyonlands is divided up among 4 sections. **Island in the Sky**, **The Maze**, & **The Needles** are all divided by the 4th section–**The Rivers**. The rapids on the Green & Colorado Rivers are some of the most intense in the country. The Maze is only reached by 4-wheel drive, so I wasn't able to make it there. The Needles was my favorite part of the park as it offers fewer crowds and endless exploration.

My favorite trail, photographed above, takes you to the rock formations called **The Needles**. I drove to **Elephant Hill** and began my 8 mile loop trail to **Chestler Park**. There were so many fantastic views and climbing over all the rocks was so much fun!

Over in **Island in the Sky** I loved the view from **Mesa Arch** photographed on the opposite page. To get the amazing 360° view shown below, hike out to the **Grand View Point**.

While there are multiple places in the country where you can see cliff dwellings, **Cliff Palace** in Mesa Verde is the most impressive. Photographed on the bottom right, this architectural feat is the main draw to this park. As the nation's 7th national park, the importance of preserving these historical artifacts was imperative.

 tarantula, king snake

Most of the heritage sites here are all accessible by an easy walk from the road. I spent one full day here and that was sufficient. Besides checking out of the historical structures, I enjoyed the 2.4 mile **Petroglyph Point Trail** offering great canyon views and the chance to see some petroglyphs.

If you like seeing historical artifacts, the visitor's center has a large portion of pottery & tools left from the cliff dwellers.

I visited this park in October, which is great for less crowds, but as it was off season for the park the entire **Wetherill Mesa** area was closed and no tours to the **Cliff Palace** or **Balcony House** were being offered.

Similar to the Grand Canyon, Black Canyon can be accessed from both the north and south rims. Most people visit the south rim as it's easy to get to, and it is more developed. I arrived at the park for sunset which was great to observe over the canyon, and then went to the nearby town for dinner. The next day after hiking down to the river and back up, I checked out the rest of the overlooks. Pictured above is **Painted Rock**. The wall is twice as tall as the Empire State Building and one of the tallest cliff walls in the country.

Inner Canyon Hiking: Gunnison Route

While a majority of the park consists of driving to different overlooks along the canyon rim, you can also hike down into the canyon to the Gunnison River. There are no official trails, and permits are required. Several wilderness routes lead down to the river and are for those with a strong sense of adventure! I arrived first thing in the morning to obtain a permit to do the Gunnison Route and the ranger told me that a couple had already attempted this route earlier but had turned back because they had encountered both a black bear and a mountain lion.

At the time it was raining so I was especially reluctant when the ranger said she didn't recommend hiking down to the river "if you want to have a good time at the park." Well my sense of adventure took over, and I started the hike down with my bear spray in hand. The route was very challenging but the sun appeared, and it turned out to be an awesome experience! On the top right you can see me pointing to the route that I took.

My favorite thing to do at the park was rent a sand board and fly down the dunes! Right outside the park there's a place to rent sleds or sand boards for having some fun in the desert!

GREAT SAND DUNES
NATIONAL PARK AND PRESERVE

NATIONAL PARK SERVICE
DEPARTMENT OF THE INTERIOR

Nearby: Zapata Falls

Located right outside the park entrance in the Rio Grande National Forest, this short 1 mile trail takes you to a sensational waterfall. There are also great places to park a van and camp in the national forest.

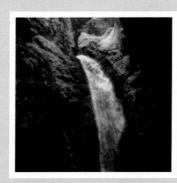

 mountain lion

The drive to this park is simply stunning as there are mountains all around. As you approach the park you can see the sand dunes from quite a distance. Once at the park there is plenty of exploring you can do in the sand dunes; however, trekking up and down the dunes is exhausting! It was my experience at the park that most people did not explore beyond the first or second mounds of sand. Just walking up and over those two mounds allowed me to find solitude in the park.

Due to the park's close proximity to Denver, Rocky Mountain National Park can get pretty crowded. The park has implemented a reservation system for entrance to help reduce the congestion.

My favorite place in the park is the 8.3 mile roundtrip hike to **Sky Pond**.

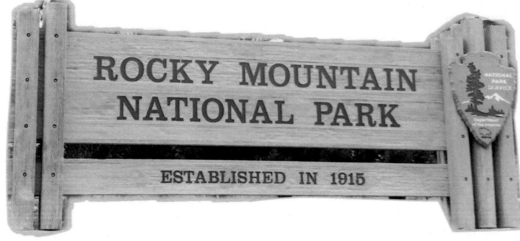

ROCKY MOUNTAIN NATIONAL PARK

ESTABLISHED IN 1915

 ELK

This park gets a lot of snow! **Trail Ridge Road** is the main road through the park and is only open from roughly June - September depending on conditions. This road reaches up to 12,000 feet above sea level. The first time I visited the park it was late April, and there was still lots of snow on the ground. The two main entrances are located in the towns of Estes Park and Grand Lake. Both areas are beautiful and going from one to the other via Trail Ridge Road would most likely take just over an hour if you weren't stopping. However, when I first went in April the road was closed and I had to drive all the way around the park, which is almost a 5 hour detour.

Favorite Hikes

Jenny Lake Trail (5-7 mi)

Take this trail to access *Inspiration Point* & *Hidden Falls*. Alternatively you can take the water taxi if you want a shorter hike.

Amphitheater Lake Trail (11 mi)

While this will be a long day hike, you will make it to 3 alpine lakes. *Amphitheater*, *Surprise*, & my favorite, *Delta Lake* are all worth the journey.

moose
fox
martin
elk
black bear
pika
pronghorn

The peaks on Teton Range are striking to see over the horizon. Photographed on the bottom of opposite page is my favorite view of the Tetons from **Schwabacher Landing**. Right outside the south entrance of the park sits Jackson, WY. This bustling little town offers great food and lodging in close proximity to some amazing scenery.

While at this park, I chose to camp at Colter Bay Campground. I was amazed at the amount of wildlife in the park, even at the campground! On the second day we were arriving back at the campsite for dinner when a black bear and her two cubs were walking right through the campsite!

Rockefeller Parkway &
Caribou-Targhee National Forest

If you're looking for a place to just relax in nature, then head to this area. Situated between Grand Teton & Yellowstone, the unpaved **Grassy Lake Road** offers excellent free camping. This drive is beautiful and there are great hiking and camping spots all along the road. My favorite thing to do here is to soak in the hot springs after a long day of hiking. While there are a ton of hot springs in the parkway, **Polecat** & **Huckleberry** hot springs are both good options for a nice soak. You will most likely have to cross the creek to access them so bring your water shoes!

Yellowstone National Park

YELLOWSTONE NATIONAL PARK

Be prepared for lots of crowds here! While this iconic park reigns as America's first national park, it comes with lots of tourists. This park is huge and getting anywhere will take some time. Between traffic jams due to bison and over-crowded parking lots, you will need some patience. I entered the south entrance first, and without stopping it took almost 4 hours just to reach the north entrance.

bison, elk, grizzly bear, bald eagle

There is no shortage of geothermal areas in the park. There are so many spots of the park worth checking out, that it is hard to recommend any specific area. While **Old Faithful** is spectacular, there are even bigger & better geysers to see especially in the **Upper Geyser Basin**. The classic rainbow colored **Prismatic Spring** is beautiful to see in person.

Since the park is so huge I wanted to camp inside the park. This proved to be frustrating as a lot of the sites are first come, first served. As the park doesn't have cell service to determine which sites have availability, I spent hours just driving around trying to find an open campsite.

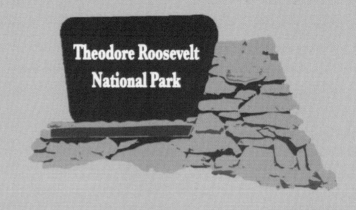

Theodore Roosevelt National Park

horses, bison, prairie dogs, short-horned lizard

Driving into North Dakota I wasn't anticipating much from this park, but I was pleasantly surprised at how cool the park was. The park is divided up among two main units, the north & south units of the park. There is a very small third unit that is only accessible by a rough dirt road called the Elkhorn Ranch unit. This is the area of Roosevelt's ranch.

I began with the north unit and this was definitely my favorite area. I enjoyed the fact that there were far less visitors and way more animals here. My favorite memory here was a sunset hike starting on the *Buckhorn Connector* and continuing on the *Buckhorn Trail* to the prairie dog town. On this trail I loved seeing the prairie dogs, and I ran into a herd of roughly 50 bison on the trail, so I had to turn around at that point. The south unit does have a great scenic loop drive offering lots of great viewpoints.

When I visited this park in 2023 all the cave tours were closed due to mechanical issues with the elevator. The natural entrance to the cave is very small, so the only way in or out is by the elevator. The small cave entrance makes a whistling sound as pressure moves in or out of the cave. Compared to Badlands which is right next door, this park had little to offer me since the cave was closed. Despite this I did enjoy going up the fire tower for a view over the park lands.

bison, prairie dog

Because of its proximity to I-90, this park is really easy to drive through one way and continue onto the highway after. While I did enjoy the drive and stopping to do some hikes, it paled in comparison to other parks nearby. This park seems fairly small for a national park, and I was able to see everything I wanted to in a day. I had arrived the evening before in the middle of a thunderstorm, so it was really incredible seeing the lightning strikes over the landscape. It was easy enough to find a pull off to park and sleep for the night. The next day was pretty warm so Mako and I just got up and enjoyed a lot of the pull-offs and did a little off-trail exploring on our own as there aren't too many trails here in the park.

 antelope, bison, prairie dog, bighorn sheep

Virgin Islands National Park

Eastern Parks

Located between USA and Canada, Voyageurs National Park is a treasure in the boundary waters. Originally home of the Ojibwe Indians now sits an area full of wilderness and wildlife. The most common activity here at the park is to canoe the waterways just like the original settlers did. They would have been hunting for food and fur, while visitors today can explore the water in search of wildlife and beautiful landscapes. Mako and I rented a canoe, and I reserved us our own private island to camp at for the night, and it was simply perfect! This park is known for being able to see the northern lights over 50% of the time!

loon, bald eagle

The only way to get to this remote island is by boat. Isle Royale is an island located in the abyss of Lake Superior. The NPS offers a ferry (*shown to the left*) from Houghton, MI which is how I got to the island. The ride over was pretty intense. The ferry takes about 6 hours and is subject to the rough waters of the lake. I experienced some of the roughest swells I've ever been in, and it wasn't even in the ocean!

I camped at this park overnight, and it was the perfect amount of time for me to explore the island and wander on a nice sunset hike. For backpackers, this park would make a great 3-4 day journey for those wanting an adventure.

 fox

isle royale national park

an international biosphere reserve

Indiana Dunes
National Park

If you are looking for a nice place to relax on a beach, then the sandy shore of the park is perfect for you. Located on Lake Michigan this lakeshore is a nice getaway from the hustle and bustle of Chicago, which is about an hour drive away.

There are a few trails in the park that meander through the dunes and forested areas of the park, but the main draw here is the sandy shore. Lake Michigan remains fairly cold all year round. I enjoyed the tranquility that I found by walking along the lakeshore. Besides enjoying an afternoon on the beach, you won't find many activities in this park.

Welcome to
**Cuyahoga
Valley**
National Park

This park offers a lot of trails to explore. While there are no grand vistas in the park, there are lots of rock formations and waterfalls to explore.

During my visit to this park I encountered some snow which was fun to hike in. I had already been to this park before doing vanlife. If I would have stopped at this park en-route to Acadia, then it would have been late fall—the perfect time for leaf peeping.

The Beehive Trail

This was my favorite trail in the park. I love how unique and challenging this trail is. The trail is only .6 miles up, but it is essentially straight up the side of the mountain. It will require you to hike along thin rock faces as well as climb up metal rungs in the side of the rocks. After reaching the top you will be rewarded with a great viewpoint and can hike down an easier path.

Located in Maine, this gorgeous stretch of coastline is a gem of the North East. The rocky shores provide unique landscapes to explore. There are lots of fantastic areas to explore in the park. **Jordan Pond** is a very scenic inland area of the park. I enjoyed the trail around the lake as well as hiking up to the **South Bubble** viewpoint for a great vista above the pond. **Cadillac Mountain** is the highest point in the park, however you must obtain a permit to drive to the top. Parking at **Sand Beach** and hiking the **Great Head** trail was my favorite place to explore the coastline with less crowds. I camped at the **Seawall Campground** for 2 nights and loved being so close to the water. Nearby the camp area is the iconic **Bass Harbor Head Lighthouse** (*photographed to the left*). The park is located around the quaint town of **Bar Harbor**. Here you will find amazing opportunities for shopping, lodging, and dining.

Skyline Drive

This park offers some amazing vistas just on the park roads, whether that is winding through the forest or stopping at a pull-off to observe the sweeping landscape. When I went to this park it was in the middle of summer, and the waterfalls felt very refreshing. I would love to come back and drive these park roads again during the fall when the leaves are all changing.

Pet Friendly

Shenandoah is a fantastic national park if you are traveling with your dog. Dogs are allowed on almost all of the park trails here with the exception of just a few trails. Only the really crowded trails are off limits to dogs to help reduce the congestion of those trails.

Mako and I did an early morning hike while the fog was still in the air. On the trail we did see a snake. There are also a lot of black bears in the park, but thankfully we didn't see any on the trails.

Mary's Rock Out-and-Back Trail

This 3.8 mile roundtrip trail offers excellent views on the rock outcroppings from Mary's Rock. This was my favorite trail that I did in the park. I also enjoyed the 1.7 mile roundtrip hike to **Dark Hollow Falls** (*photographed to the right*) to cool off in the frigid waters.

snake

SHENANDOAH
NATIONAL PARK
U.S. DEPARTMENT OF THE INTERIOR
NATIONAL PARK SERVICE

America's newest national park, New River Gorge changed status from a national river to a national park in 2020. There are many ways to enjoy this park such as camping, hiking, white water rafting, climbing, biking, horse-back riding, and so much more. Additionally, this park is super **pet friendly** as dogs are allowed on all the trails at this park.

Some of my favorite spots in the park include seeing the cascades (*pictured below*) at **Sandstone Falls**, admiring the vista at **Grandview Overlook**, gazing at the iconic bridge from **Long Point Overlook**, or hiking the **Endless Wall Trail**.

Established in 1941, the Mammoth cave system is the largest in the entire world. In order to experience these underground passageways, you will need to go on a ranger led tour. There are multiple tour options depending on your time and abilities. As you can see from the photo below, there are signs of human activity in the caves that can be traced over 2,000 years ago. While there are some trails here, below the surface is where it's at.

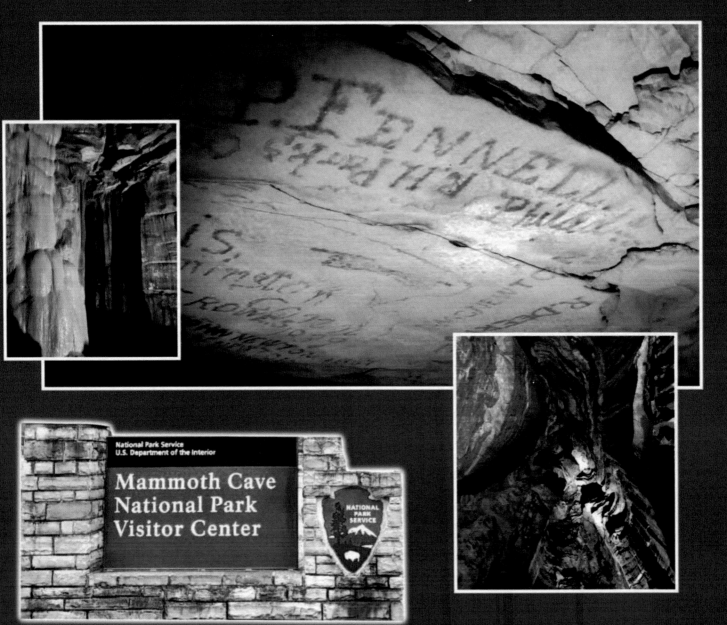

National Park Service
U.S. Department of the Interior

Mammoth Cave
National Park
Visitor Center

NATIONAL
PARK
SERVICE

This park was preserved mainly for its historical significance. While the name sounds appealing, you can't actually soak in any hot springs in nature as you might expect from a national park. Instead, eight bathhouses were built in the late 1800s so that consumers could utilize the steamy water. While not all of the bathhouses are operable anymore, you can still relax in one of the open bathhouses for a fee.

Additionally, there are some hiking trails in the park, but they aren't anything of significance. There is a tower in the park, and I enjoyed the view from the tower photographed here.

Gateway Arch received national park status in 2018 making it one of the newest national parks by congress. While you won't find hiking trails here, the grounds make for a great city park in downtown St. Louis, Missouri.

I've had the opportunity to visit this park in the fall as well as in the winter. The fall is a great time of year to enjoy laying on the lawn and have a picnic lunch. In contrast, the park is transformed into a winter wonderland blanketed in snow in the early months of the year. Mako especially loved playing in the snow on a cold winter afternoon. Dogs are welcome on the grounds here just not inside the buildings.

The arch towers above the Mississippi River at 630 feet above the ground. In fact, you can even take the 4 minute tram ride all the way up the curve of the arch to the top observation deck for a sweeping view of the city.

The arch symbolizes the west bound expansion and exploration through St. Louis during the 1800s.

Great Smoky Mountains National Park

National Park Service
U.S. Department of the Interior

Growing up in South Carolina I've had the opportunity to visit this park in every season. No matter when you choose to visit the Smokey Mountains it will always be beautiful. This national park brings in more visitors annually than any other national park in the country. That being said, expect crowds! One of my favorite areas of the park is the **Cades Cove Scenic Loop**. Driving this loop you will have a high likelihood of spotting a black bear. My suggestion is to go early morning! Not only will you have a better chance of seeing a bear, but you will also avoid heavy congestion on the road. There are also lots of great waterfalls scattered throughout the park for you to experience. This is one of the only parks that spans between multiple states–TN and NC.

elk, black bear, turkey

WESTON LAKE LOOP
OAKRIDGE TRAIL
KINGSNAKE TRAIL

WILDERNESS BOUNDARY

lots of snakes!

National Park Service
U.S. Department of the Interior

Congaree
National Park

NATIONAL
PARK
SERVICE

If adventure is what you want, then this park is perfect for you. Expect hot humid weather, muddy or swampy trails, and lots of mosquitoes! Often the hiking trails are flooded turning them into kayaking trails. I knew this ahead of time so I brought my kayak and enjoyed paddling down the trails.

The best way to experience this park is by boat. 95% of the park boundaries are in the ocean. There are a lot of activities you can do here such as fishing, snorkeling, kayaking, or sailing. The national park has a visitors center that you can drive to in under an hour from Miami. From there, I chose one of the tour operators to take me out on a boat to snorkel one of the shipwrecks out on a reef.

dolphin, eel, barracuda, tropical fish, pelican, lizard, Man-o-war jellyfish

Biscayne National Park

While this is the tenth largest park in America, most of the park is inaccessible unless you plan to wade through the alligator filled swamplands. There are four different visitor centers to access depending on where in Florida you are coming from. Driving south from Miami you will reach the Ernest F. Coe visitor center in about an hour. From here you will be able to access most of the hiking trails within the park. If hiking isn't on your agenda, consider taking an airboat ride to experience a large portion of this wilderness at high speeds!

alligator, manatee, roseate spoonbill, egret, ibis, osprey, heron, striped mud turtle

In my opinion, this is one of the most beautiful
islands in the Caribbean. Sure a lot of islands in
the area have pretty vistas and clear waters, but St.
John is an island free of resorts and development.
Seeing the beautiful landscapes throughout the
island with no buildings makes this island special. I
can't really recommend any one specific area of
the park to explore, because I enjoyed all of the
beaches and trails in this park. No matter where
your national park exploration takes you within
the park, you will be amazed at its beauty. I do
recommend renting a car in St. Thomas and
taking the car ferry over that way you can explore
most of the park with ease. Just keep in mind you
will be driving on the left side of the road!

VIRGIN ISLANDS NATIONAL PARK

United States Department of the Interior
National Park Service

Snorkeling in the clear waters around the park was the highlight of my visit. Tons of marine life thrive on the reefs just off shore. There are multiple areas around the park to lay out on a nice sandy beach or dive into the water to see an entirely new landscape waiting to be discovered. The area I saw the most sea turtles in was snorkeling at **Francis Bay**.

sea turtle
tropical fish
soldier crab
pelican

This was my last national park to visit, and I thoroughly enjoyed it! In order to get to the park you will either have to take the ferry or a float place from Key West. While both options are pricey, they ferry will save on costs. There is only one ferry per day, and it departs from Key West at 8am and returns to town around 5:30pm. That means your time on the island will be from 10:30am - 3pm. For me, I was so glad that I chose to stay the night and camp on the island. Not only were the stars amazing, but after the ferry departed, I basically had the island to myself other than a few other campers and the rangers. It was spectacular watching the sunset from the fort.

The blue waters around the island make for great snorkeling! Here you will find a wide variety of marine life while out exploring the ocean. There are also nice sandy beaches to relax on!

sea turtle
eagle ray
grouper
tropical fish
manatee
pelican
barracuda

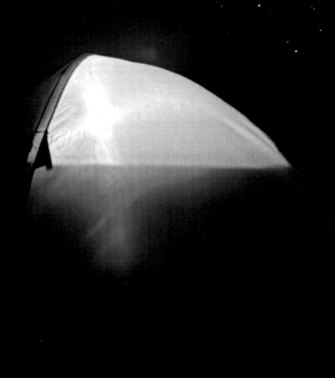

Vanlife Tip

In order to get to Dry Tortugas National Park, you will have to leave your van or car in Key West near the ferry terminal. The website says that the only parking is located in the parking garage across the street. However, the garage charges $40/day. I parked my van about two blocks away from the terminal on the street for free. I didn't have any issues parking here overnight while I was camping.

_____'s National Park Checklist

- [ ] Acadia
- [ ] Arches
- [ ] Badlands
- [ ] Big Bend
- [ ] Biscayne
- [ ] Black Canyon of the Gunnison
- [ ] Bryce Canyon
- [ ] Canyonlands
- [ ] Capitol Reef
- [ ] Carlsbad Caverns
- [ ] Channel Islands
- [ ] Congaree
- [ ] Crater Lake
- [ ] Cuyahoga Valley
- [ ] Death Valley
- [ ] Denali
- [ ] Dry Tortugas
- [ ] Everglades
- [ ] Gates of the Arctic
- [ ] Gateway Arch
- [ ] Glacier

- [ ] Glacier Bay
- [ ] Grand Canyon
- [ ] Grand Teton
- [ ] Great Basin
- [ ] Great Sand Dunes
- [ ] Great Smokey Mountains
- [ ] Guadalupe Mountains
- [ ] Haleakala
- [ ] Hawaii Volcanoes
- [ ] Hot Springs
- [ ] Indiana Dunes
- [ ] Isle Royale
- [ ] Joshua Tree
- [ ] Katmai
- [ ] Kenai Fjords
- [ ] Kings Canyon
- [ ] Kobuk Valley
- [ ] Lake Clark
- [ ] Lassen Volcanic
- [ ] Mammoth Cave
- [ ] Mesa Verde

- [ ] Mount Rainier
- [ ] National Park of American Samoa
- [ ] New River Gorge
- [ ] North Cascades
- [ ] Olympic
- [ ] Petrified Forest
- [ ] Pinnacles
- [ ] Redwoods
- [ ] Rocky Mountain
- [ ] Saguaro
- [ ] Sequoia
- [ ] Shenandoah
- [ ] Theodore Roosevelt
- [ ] Virgin Islands
- [ ] Voyageurs
- [ ] White Sands
- [ ] Wind Cave
- [ ] Wrangell-St. Elias
- [ ] Yellowstone
- [ ] Yosemite
- [ ] Zion